Learn How to play the Bluegrass Way

ASAP

Beginning
Bluegrass Banjo

By Ron Middlebrook
with Dick Sheridan

To access audio visit:
www.halleonard.com/mylibrary

Enter Code
2116-6001-7513-8125

ISBN 978-1-57424-381-9
SAN 683-8022

Cover by James Creative Group

Copyright © 2019 CENTERSTREAM Publishing
P.O. Box 17878 - Anaheim Hills, CA 92817

www.centerstream-usa.com | centerstrm@aol.com | 714-779-9390

TABLE OF CONTENTS

A WORD FROM THE AUTHOR

The task of this book is to teach you, the reader, how to play bluegrass 5-string banjo. Even if you've never played before -- what some teachers refer to as a "tabula rasa (a blank slate) -- you'll find all the necessary steps to begin your playing experience.

We'll start from the bottom up. First we'll examine the banjo itself, name all its parts, then look at some of the accessories you'll need to play. We'll introduce a simplified way of reading music for the banjo called tablature. A few standard music terms are also necessary and we'll check those out as well.

Rolls are the lifeblood of banjo playing. These are prescribed patterns of strings to be played by the right hand (assuming you're right handed) and which fingers to be correctly used. We'll study the most commonly used rolls and add a few embellishments called hammer-ons, pull-offs, and slides.

Armed with this information we can now start putting all these techniques to use and begin playing songs. We'll start off with easy songs, analyze how they're put together, then advance to more challenging ones. These songs will be drawn from the wellspring of roots music -- old-time ballads and material currently popular with bluegrass bands around the world.

We'll take some side trips to explore different tunings, see how chords are used to accompany songs, and discover breaks and fills -- musical cliches -- that are commonly worked into songs.

All in all, there's much exciting ground to be covered and we'll do it step by step, systematically, with measured strides, always with the goal of making you the best possible player ever. Developing your talent and skill is ourt foremost objective

So let's begin. Tune up, put on your finger picks, and let's start playing. Choose a song, and off we'll go. We've much material at hand for current enjoyment, and the door is wide open for new discoveries down the line. The word is out: a new bluegrass banjo player is on the scene. That player is you!

~*~

Beginning Bluegrass Banjo
ALPHABETICAL LISTING OF SONGS

INTRODUCTION
"Ring, ring the banjo, I like those good old songs ..."

Maybe it was Alison Krauss and her band *Union Station*. Maybe it was Ricky Skaggs and *Rolling Thunder*. Perhaps the sound of "Dueling Banjos" played by Eric Weissberg in the movie *Deliverance* or Earl Scruggs playing his energized composition "Foggy Mountain Breakdown" in the film *Bonnie & Clyde*.

It could have been Bela Fleck, Tony Trischka, or comedian Steve Martin. A good chance it might have been the recordings of *Old And In The Way* or maybe even the soundtrack from the 2000 movie *O Brother, Where Art Thou.*

Wherever, the sound was unmistakable. Hard driving, soaring vocals, dynamic instrumentation. No mistaking that sound. Clearly identifiable. Bluegrass!

It all began in the hills and back country of Appalachia where Celtic ballads were preserved and passed on to rural singers and musicians. These traditional songs were the inspiration for early bands and instrumentalists, and the mountains and "hollers" echoed with their sound.

It was only natural that musicians would gather and play together. String bands gradually emerged and acquired identity. But of all those early groups none shaped the sound more distinctively than Bill Monroe's 1945 *Blue Grass Boys* consisting of Bill on mandolin, Lester Flatt on guitar, Chubby Wise playing fiddle, Howard Watts on bass, and a young 24-year-old banjo player, Earl Scruggs, who would revolutionize the banjo world with his unique virtuostic style. Bill was from Kentucky, the Bluegrass State, and hence the name of his band.

Flatt and Scruggs spun off from the Monroe band in 1948 to form what was to become another iconic bluegrass band, the *Foggy Mountain Boys* – not to be confused with the hilarious fictional *Soggy Bottom Boys* from the *O Brother, Where Art Thou* movie.

Many bands soon adopted the classic Monroe format with the same kind of acoustic instruments and vocal harmony. Notable among those early bands was the *Stanley Brothers* and their group *The Clinch Mountain Boys*. It's interesting to note that banjo player Ralph Stanley was originally a 2-finger player who later switched to the 3-finger style popularized by Earl Scruggs.

Another influential early band was the *Osborne Brothers* known especially for their 1967 recording of "Rocky Top." About the same time from the Washington, D.C. area came the *Country Gentlemen* and their signature song "Fox On The Run" released in 1972.

Ralph Stanley and Sonny Osborne, along with other early players like Don Reno from the *Tennessee Cut-Ups*, can be credited with inspiring a dynasty of well-known banjo players that includes Bill Keith, Noam Pikelny, J.D. Crowe, Alan Munde, John Hartford, Jim Mills and Peter Wernick, to name only a few among the many.

Bluegrass festivals, concerts, and recordings ignited younger generations of players, and as the country caught bluegrass fever new bands emerged -- groups like *Old And In The Way*, the *Del McCoury Band*, *Nickel Creek*, and the *Seldom Scene*. And as is the way of evolution, different approaches to playing bluegrass began to appear. Called newgrass and progressive, these altered styles broke the mold of playing only traditional music with just traditional instruments.

The influences on bluegrass have come from many sources and musicians, but primarily it all goes back to Bill Monroe, rightly called "The Father of Bluegrass." He set the stage, established the format, and inspired generations of performers and listeners.

 The following pages will help you on your way to join the ranks of bluegrass banjo players. You'll find a solid foundation of essentials and a repertoire of some of the best songs in the bluegrass tradition. The pathway ahead leads to a world of endless fun and fascination, and it's yours for the taking.

Bluegrass lives! And the bluegrass baton now passes to you.

Snuffy Jenkins with Flat & Scruggs - 1968

BANJO PARTS

Peghead: top of the banjo where the 4 Tuning Pegs (tuners) are located.

Nut: the thin piece of wood, bone, or plastic between the peghead and fingerboard over which the strings pass in slotted grooves.

Neck: the "arm" of the banjo that extends from the peghead to the pot.

Fingerboard: sits on top of the neck from the nut to end of the neck. It is also called a fretboard.

Frets: thin metal wires, usually 21, that divide the fretboard. The spaces beween the metal frets can also be called "Frets" and are sometimes inlaid with pearl dots or ornate designs called position markers.

Side Dots: small white dots on the side of the neck that serve as position markers.

Head: a plastic or animal skin that covers the top of the pot.

Bridge: a thin wooden "tressel" resting on the head over which the strings pass in slotted grooves.

Pot: the hoop, the drum.

Tension band and brackets: used to pull down the head and tighten it.

Tone Ring: various configurations of a metal ring that fits under the head. Can be solid, tubular, or angled, with or without holes. Not all banjos have tone rings.

Resonator: the covering plate for the back of the pot. Originally pie plates were used.

Tailpiece: anchors the end of the strings to the pot.

Arm Rest: a metal or wood support for the right hand attached to the rim of the pot

5th String peg: a separate tuner for the 5th string located close to the 5th fret.

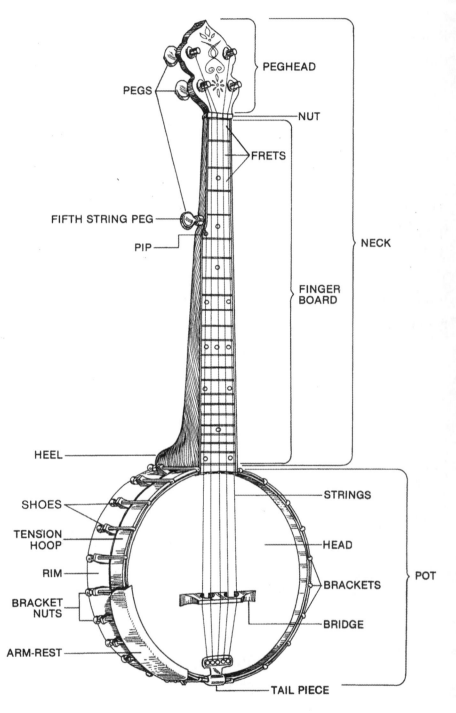

THE GEAR

FINGER PICKS

Although the banjo can be played with bare fingers, bluegrass players typically use finger picks for the thumb, index, and middle fingers of the right hand. These picks can be made from metal or plastic depending on the sound preference of the player. A popular combination is a plastic pick for the thumb with metal picks for the index and middle fingers. It should be mentioned that these metal picks should curl under the finger tips not above like claws.

STRINGS

Banjo strings can be metal or nylon. Nylon is preferred for some antique instruments so that too much pressure is not put on the neck possibly causing it to warp. Nylon strings are tied with a knot to the tailpiece. Metal strings are manufactured with either a ball end (or grommet) or a loop. The gauge or thickness of the string can vary from light to heavy, the choice being the preference of the player. Manufacturers vary in their choice of string thickness but a typical light selection might be .095-.010-.013-.020 wound-.095. The 1st and 5th string are often the same gauge, the 4th string sometimes wound. Metal strings usually are stainless steel, silver plated steel, and nickel wound.

CASES

Protect your banjo with either a hard shell case or soft, padded "gig" bag. Cases are great places to store music, extra strings, tools, picks, etc. Match the value of the instrument with the quality of the case.

STRAPS

If you're a standup player you'll need a strap, and there are many kinds to choose from. If you sit when you play try putting a chamois or rubberized shelf liner on your lap to prevent the banjo from sliding.

THE CAPO

To change the pitch of the banjo without retuning the strings, a device called a capo (pronounced KAY-po) is used. There are two kinds, a 4-string capo and a 5th string capo. Essentially a clamp, the 4-string capo places a bar across all the stings except the 5th and can be moved up or down the neck. This allows songs to be played in different keys without changing the original way the song is arranged. In addition to

Stub B Capo   *5th String Sliding Capo*   *Railroad Spike*

the clamped bar, the 5th string must be moved accordingly. A capo on the 2nd fret would require the 5th string to be moved up two frets. The 5th string can be capoed by using an "L" shaped spike used to hold down the tracks of model railroads. The string is tucked under the spike which is "nailed" into the fingerboard at different frets. Another style of capo is a narrow bar attached to the side of the neck on which a "finger" can be slid up or down on the 5th string. Yet another style of 5th string capo is a movable clamp that wraps around the back of the banjo neck and extends only over the 5th string. There is also a capo that attaches directly to the 5th string; it uses a thumb screw to put pressure on a small metal piece that can be slid up or down the string.

TUNING THE BANJO

Most of the songs in this book are played in G tuning. Here's how the strings are tuned:

1st string   - D
2nd string - B
3rd string   - G
4th string   - D
5th string   - g

The tuning for each song is written in the upper left hand corner of the song. For G tuning it would be written: gDGBD. The small "g" indicates the high pitch of the 5th string. The D strings are spaced an octave apart, the 4th string a lower D, the 1st string a higher D. The word "octave" is a musical term meaning eight notes.

There are other popular tunings that are also used in this book. Like G tuning they are listed in the string order 5-4-3-2-1.

C tuning - gCGBD, Modal tuning - gDGCD, and D tuning - f#-DF#AD

Unless you have "perfect pitch" (the ability to identify or sing at will a musical sound by name) you'll need some sort of reference to tune each string correctly. If you tune by ear this is called "relative pitch" and it means matching the string to some source of sound like a piano or other instrument, a tuning fork or pitch pipe. Far easier and far more accurate is the use of a digital (electronic) tuner that attaches to the banjo and displays the letter name of the pitch. Some of these tuners are "dedicated" just to the banjo or some other specific instrument. Another style of tuner is called "chromatic." It displays all 12 tones of the musical scale and can be used for any instrument.

BANJO FINGERBOARD CHART
G TUNING

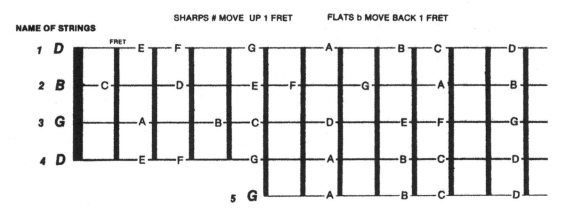

TUNERS

Tuning the banjo was once limited to matching pitches with a tuning fork, a piano or some other instrument, or to a pitch pipe that you would blow into. These methods required a good ear as do some online tuners currently available on the computer. Times have changed and digital tuners have become the norm. These tuners -- and there are many styles -- have a graphic display that shows the letter name of the string and indicates whether the string is in tune or too low (flat) or high (sharp). Tuners range in price from below $20 to several hundred dollars. Some tuners are free standing while others clip on the banjo. Some produce an audible pitch.

Without the use of a digital tuner or matching string pitch to another instrument or source of pitch, the banjo can be tuned "to itself" in a manner called Relative Tuning:

    (1) The low 4th string is tuned by ear to what is assumed to be a D, right or wrong. Just get a good low sound from the string.

    (2) Play the note on the 5th fret of the 4th string and match the open 3rd string to it.

    (3) Now play the 4th fret on the 3rd string and match the open 2nd string to it.

    (4) Next on the 2nd string play the 3rd fret and match the open 1st string. to it.

    (5) Lastly play the 5th fret on the 1st string and tune the open 5th string to that pitch.

TABLATURE

Music for the 5-string banjo is written in a systems called tablature, or TAB for short. It's a way of showing you where to place your fingers without actually knowing the names of the notes you're playing.

This simplified method of writing music goes back hundred of years to the days of the lute. It consists of five horizontal lines called a staff, each line representing a string of the banjo. We'll number these lines 5-4-3-2-1, the bottom line of the staff being the banjo's high 5th string.

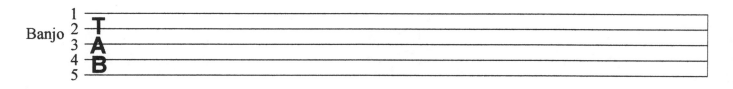

Here are the string numbers and the name of the pitch they're tuned to:

$$1 = \text{high D}$$
$$2 = \text{B}$$
$$3 = \text{G}$$
$$4 = \text{low D}$$
$$5 = \text{high G}$$

Fingers are placed on these strings to produce different sounds. An open string without any fingers on it is marked with an 0. If a first fret is called for a number 1 is placed on the string. A second fret would be indicated by a 2, a third fret by a 3, and so on up the finger-board.

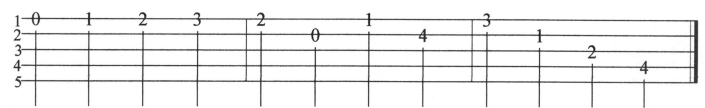

In the first measure above all of the frets are played on the 1st string.
In the second measure the frets are played on the 1st and 2nd strings.
In the third measure frets are played on all four strings.
The 5th string is usually played open.

MEASURES

Music is divided into compartments called measures. For our
purposes each of these measures will contain either three or
four beats. A beat is like the tick of a clock, a tap of the foot,
a clap of the hand, a pulse.

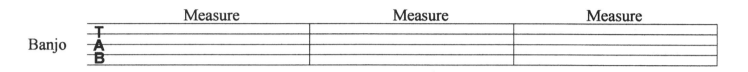

These measures contain 4 beats each:

These mesures contain three beats each:

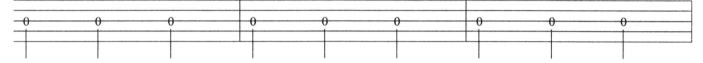

Beats can be divided:

A line of measures is called a STAFF. There are four staves (the plural of staff) on this
page. Sometimes smalll numbers appear at the beginning of a staff to identify measures.

Most songs in this book are written in 4/4 time which means 4 beats to the measure.
A song like *All The Good Times Are Past And Gone* is writen in 3/4 time which means
3 beats to the measure.

A vertical line that descends from a note head is called a stem. Notes with a single stem
get one beat. Notes connected at the bottom with a heavy line (called a beam) are
played faster. Two connected notes equal one beat. Four connected notes equal two
beats. Eight connected notes equal four beats.

A measure can also be called a BAR. The Boogie Woogie expression "Beat me, daddy,
eight to the bar" refers to playing eight notes to the measure, and those notes would be
fast.

TIMING

Notes consist of a NOTE HEAD and a vertical line callled a STEM. Notes with a single stem get one beat each. PINCHES play two notes together, usually the 1st and 5th string, and each pinch gets one beat. The following examples are in 4/4 time meaning 4 beats to the measure.

Faster notes are connected on the bottom with a heavy line called a BEAM. These can be divided into units of 2 notes for a lead/answer, 4 notes for a four-note roll, and 8 notes for an eight-note roll.

A broken roll (interrupted roll) combines a single note with a 6 note roll.

When hammer-ons, pull-offs, and slides are called for, a double beam indicates very fast notes. A slide, hammer-on or pull-off with a single beam is played slower.

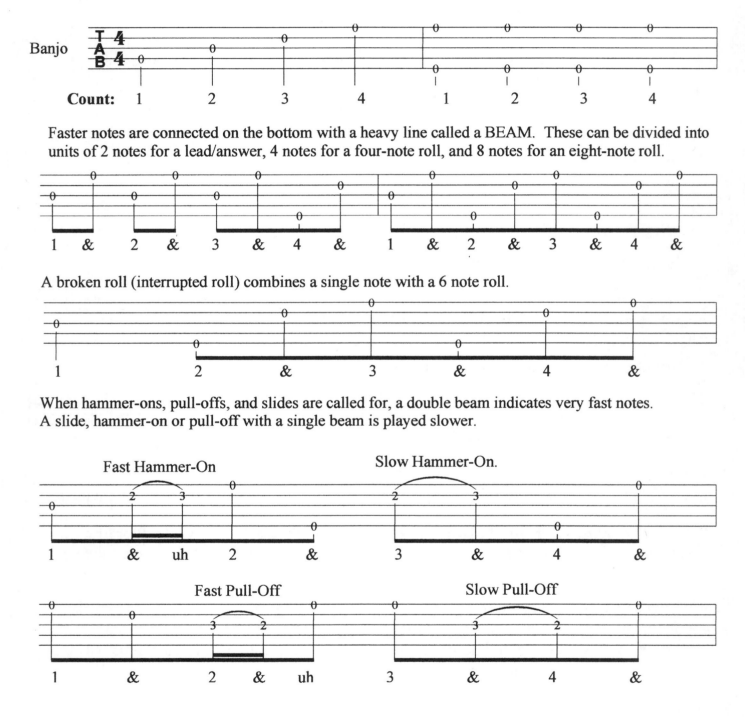

14

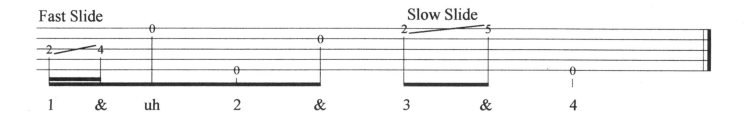

TEMPO: The speed at which a song is to be played.
At the top of each song in the upper left hand corner there's a symbol that looks like this: ♩=**120**
The numbers correspond to metronome settings and indicate how many beats there are per minute.
The tempo settings in this book are set for learning and might be played faster in actual performance.

Doug Dillard

THE SINGLE NOTE

Represented by a vertical line that descends from the note head and not connected to other notes, the single note plays a vital part in bluegrass music. Although bluegrass is typically played fast there does come a time to slow down, and that's the function of the single note. In this book it will be held for one beat but in the following examples several are held for extra beats indicated by an asterisk. Notes connected with a heavy line called a beam are played faster. The following examples all have four beats in a measure. For a detailed look at TIMING see that section in this book.

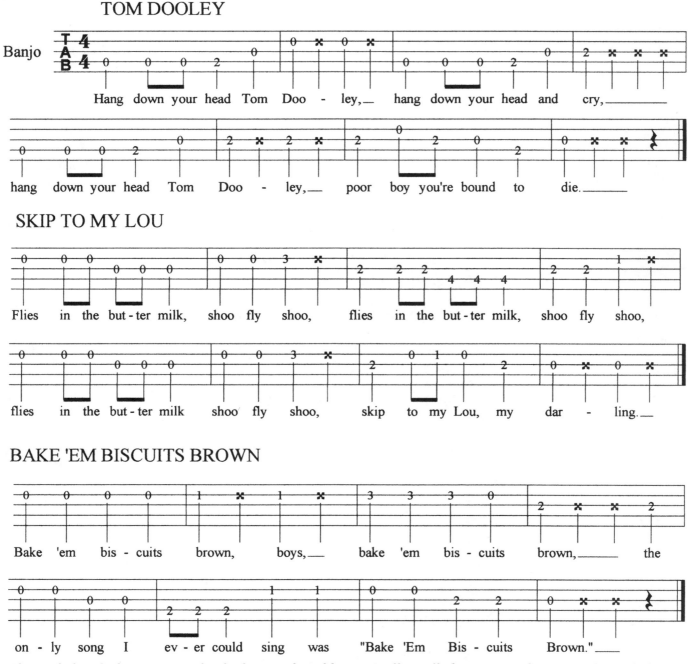

The symbol in the last measure that looks something like a seagull is called a rest. It indicates one beat of silence.

LEAD/ANSWER

Next to the single note the lead/answer is the most basic motion of the right hand. It simply consists of playing a note then following it usually with the 1st string. The lead is played with the thunb -- even if the lead is on the 2nd string which typically is played with the index finger -- then the lst string is played with the middle finger.

Banjo
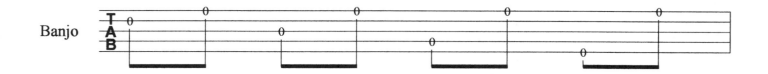

Occasionally the string order is reversed with the lead being the 1st string and the answering note the 5th string. (See the song "Fire on the Mountain" in Section Three.)

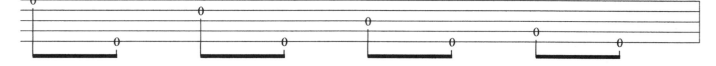

The answering note may also be a string other than the 1st.

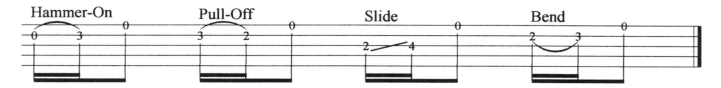

One of the "embellishment" techniques (discussed in a later section) can also be the lead.

| Hammer-On | Pull-Off | Slide | Bend |

17

THE ROLLS

Rolls are a sequence of strings that are played in a definite order. Essentially there are two kinds of rolls, one using four notes, the other eight notes.

FOUR NOTE ROLLS: Sometimes called "Scruggs" rolls since they were popularized by banjoist Earl Scruggs. The first note can be called a "lead" and is often a melody note. We'll indicate it with the letter "L" in the examples that follow. The other roll numbers reflect the string number. The low D string is number 4, the G string is 3, the B string is 2, and the high D is 1. The 5th string is marked with a 5.

As a general rule, the thumb plays the 5th, 4th, and 3rd string while the index finger plays the 2nd string and the middle finger plays the 1st string. With the exception of the 2-Finger Roll and the Variation Roll, all the other rolls are played with thee fingers.

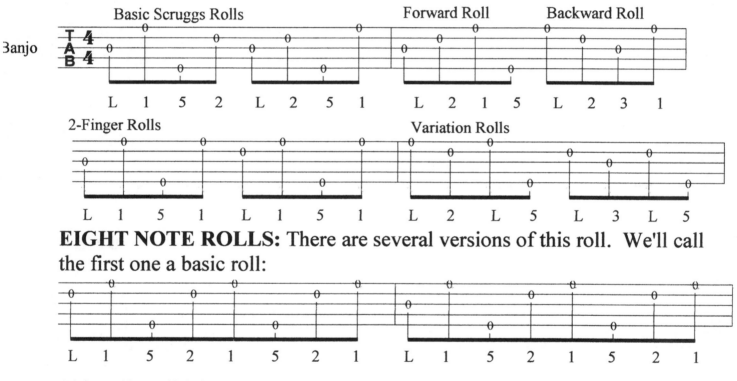

EIGHT NOTE ROLLS: There are several versions of this roll. We'll call the first one a basic roll:

This roll we'll label an "interrupted" or "broken" roll because the second note marked with an "x" is eliminated. It looks like this:

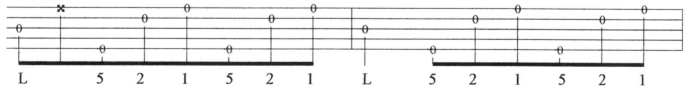

Another type of 8-note roll could be called "cascading" because of the descending notes within the roll:

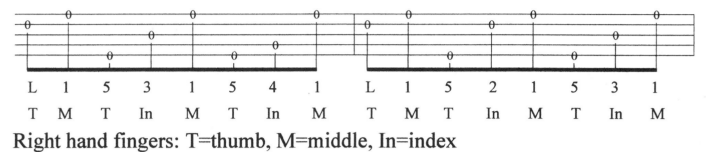

L	1	5	3	1	5	4	1	L	1	5	2	1	5	3	1
T	M	T	In	M	T	In	M	T	M	T	In	M	T	In	M

Right hand fingers: T=thumb, M=middle, In=index

A "spread" roll avoids playing the 2nd string unless it's a lead.

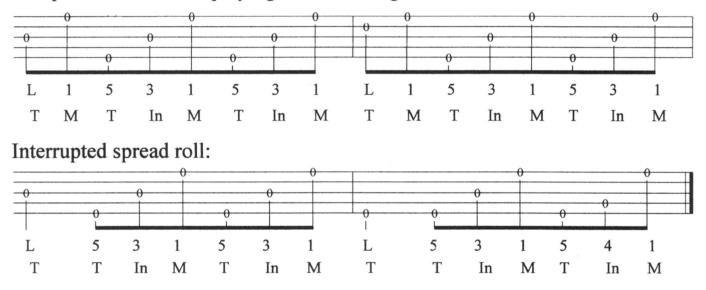

L	1	5	3	1	5	3	1	L	1	5	3	1	5	3	1
T	M	T	In	M	T	In	M	T	M	T	In	M	T	In	M

Interrupted spread roll:

L	5	3	1	5	3	1	L	5	3	1	5	4	1
T	T	In	M	T	In	M	T	T	In	M	T	In	M

Todd Taylor

19

TECHNIQUES FOR THE 5-STRING BANJO

Brush: All 5 strings are played together with a downward strum by the thumb. If finger picks are not being worn the index or middle finger could also be used.

Pinch: The middle finger picks up on the 1st string while the thumb plays the 5th string. Both strings are played together at the same time. The pinch is usually preceded by a single note but it could also be a hammer-on, pull-off or slide.

Hammer-On: This is a 2-for-1 technique in which 2 notes are sounded but the string is only picked once. The first note is played by picking the string, the second note is sounded by a finger coming down hard on a higher fret without picking the string again. The sequence is always from a low fret to a higher one, or from an open string to a fret. Hammer-ons can be played slow or fast. A double beam indicates a fast motion. In this book a curved line always appears above a hammer-on.

The first example is a confusing way of writing a hammer-on. It is the same as the following example.

Pull-Off: Like the hammer-on, the pull-off sounds 2 notes but only picks the string once. A fretted note is played and then by snapping it sideways to a lower fret on the same string (or to an open string) a second note is sounded. Pull-offs and hammer-ons are indicated in this book by a curved arc over two notes. Pull-offs always go from a high note to a lower one. Hammer-ons go from a low note to a higher one.

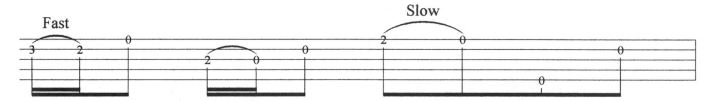

Slide: The important note of a slide is the ending note. Keep pressure on the starting note and don't be too quick in releasing the ending note. It's not important where the slide begins but where it ends. Be careful not to overshoot or undershoot the ending note since this is usually a melody note. A slide is indicate by a diagonal line between two notes. Slides are usually from a low note to a higher one but the order can be reversed.

Upward slides   Downward slides

BENDS: By pushing a string sideways and stretching it, the pitch is raised. This is also called a "choke" and is more often used with guitars than banjos.

Osborne Brothers

INTRO, BREAKS, FILLS AND TAGS

Breaks can be used as fills within a song or often as tags at the end of a song. These breaks are for songs in the key of G. Abbreviations: H-O = hammer-on, P-O = pull-off, SL= slide, T = thumb, In = index, M = middle.

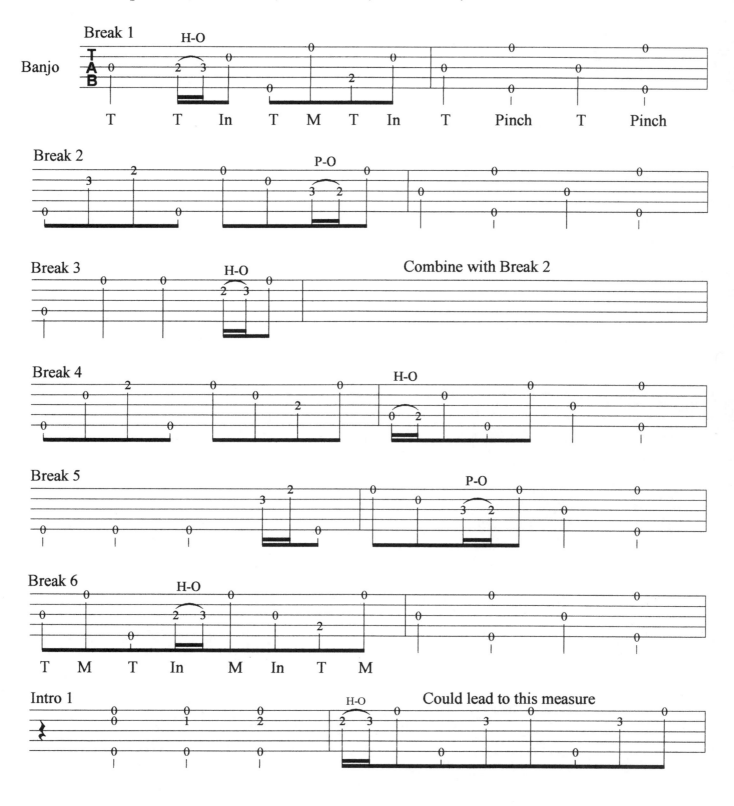

Intro 2 (pick-up)

could lead to this measure

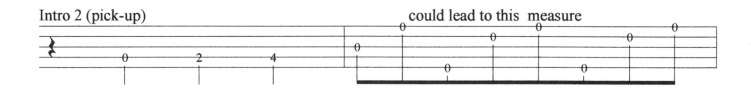

Intro 3 (pick-up)

H-O   could lead to this meassure   P-O

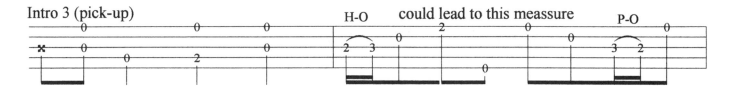

Tag 1

P-O

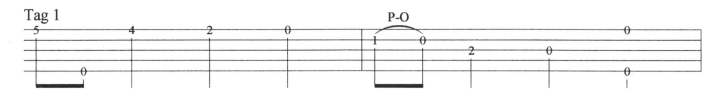

Tag 2

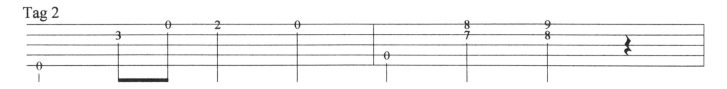

Tag 3

P-O   P-O   SL

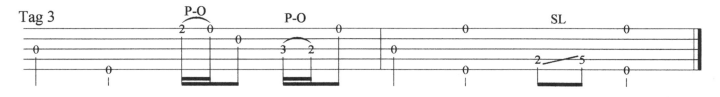

Paddygrass

ACCOMPANIMENT

Playing back-up to other instruments or vocals (yours or someone else's), is an essential part of bluegrass banjo. You'll notice alphabet letters, some with numbers, above the tablature staff. These are symbols for chords. Diagrams for the chords used in this book are included in a later section.

Accompaniment chords can be played in various ways. Here are some examples.

Four-Note Rolls: In songs where each measure has four beats, two basic 4-note rolls can be played. Suggested alternating lead strings for each roll are show in the following chart.

CHORD	LEAD STRINGS
G chord	3 and 4
C chord	4 and 3
F chord	4 and 3
Em chord	4 and 3
D7 chord	3 and 4
A7 chord	3 and 4
B7 chord	4 and 3

Eight-Note Rolls: Use the lead strings as shown above.

Note-Pinches: In measures with four beats use two note-pinches. In a measure with three beats use a note and two pinches.

Mixed: In a four-beat measure try mixing a note-pinch with a 4-note roll, or alternating measures consisting entirely of only note-pinches or 4-note rolls.

Strums: Four strums for measures with four beats. Create an "off beat" sound by strumming on the 1st and 3rd beats and resting on the 2nd and 4th beats -- or reverse the order, rest-srum-rest-strum. Three strums for measures with three beats.

There may be one or more measures where a new chord is not indicated. When that occurs continue to play the last chord shown. Some measures have two chords and these are called split measures. Play any combination for each chord that equals 2 beats, such as a two single notes, a 4-note roll, a lead-pinch, or two lead/answers.

~*~

5-STRING BANJO CHORDS
Used in this book
G tuning: gDGBD

The 5th string is not always harmonic (in tune) with the chord. When it is, an "O" will be indicated next to the string diagram. When it is not, an "X" will be shown. Even when the 5th string is not harmonic it is usually played, the discord being part of the distinctive bluegrass sound. The G chord is played "open" and requires no fingers of the left hand. The F chord shows and open circle on the 4th string. Playing that string is optional. If it is played add the 3rd fret.

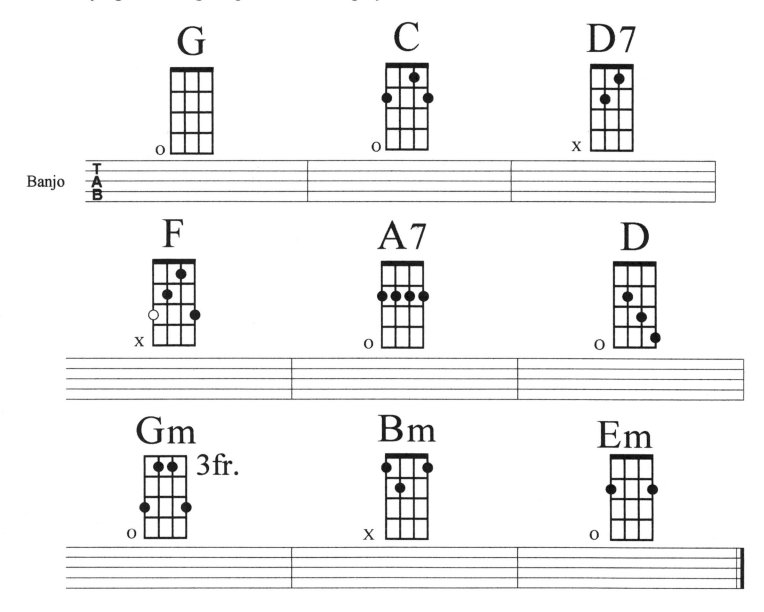

PLAYING STYLES OF THE 5-STRING BANJO

Three-Finger: This is the most popular style for bluegrass playing. It uses the thumb, index and middle fingers of the right hand. The thumb (T) can play the 5th, 4th, 3rd, and 2nd strings. The index (pointing) finger (In) is mostly used for the 2nd string, although it can reach to other strings. The middle finger (M) is dedicated to playing just the 1st string.

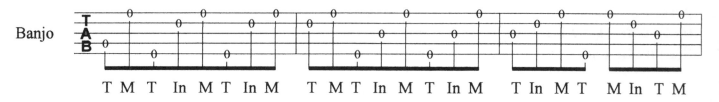

T M T In M T In M   T M T In M T In M   T In M T   M In T M

Two-Finger: Forerunner of bluegrass, uses only the thumb and index (or middle) fingers.

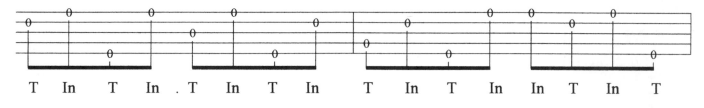

T In T In . T In T In   T In T In   In T In T

Frailing/Clawhammer: Known by both names, the nail of the middle or index finger strikes down on a string then strikes the same string again (or a different one) followed by the thumb on the 5th string. The rhythm is "bum ditty", the count 1-2/&.

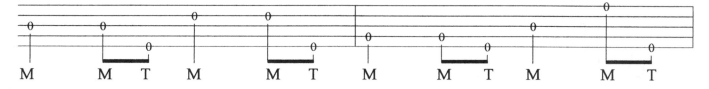

M   M T   M   M T   M   M T   M   M T

Drop-Thumb Frailing/Clawhammer: Unlike basic frailing/clawhammer where the thumb plays only the 5th string, this style finds the thumb playing additional strings. The rhythm is now "bumpa-ditty" with a count of 1/&2/&.

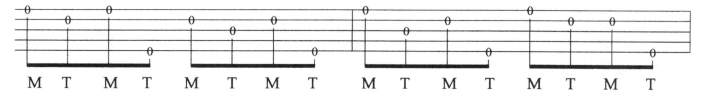

M T M T M T M T   M T M T M T M T

Up-Picking: The rhythm is the same as basic frailing/clawhammer. The index or middle finger picks up on a string then the same finger brushes all the strings in a downward motion followed by the thumb on the 5th string. The count is 1-2/&, slow-quick/quick, and can be shown as Up-Brush/Thumb. Drop-Thumbing can be added.

Up-Picking

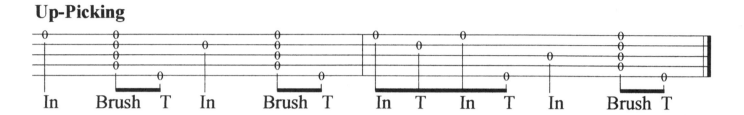

In   Brush T   In   Brush T   In T   In T   In   Brush T

Classical: Played with bare fingers, not picks, and primarily with nylon strings, this style demands skill in reading standard notation. All fingers are used except the little finger which some players rest on the head to brace the hand. Espoused by the *American Banjo Fraternity,* its members are dedicated, relatively few, and highly disciplined.

SECTION ONE

In this section the focus will be on 4-note rolls. Supporting techniques include hammer-ons, pull-offs, and slides, along with single notes and pinches. The songs will range from easy to slightly more advanced in both 3-finger and 2-finger styles. Ample tips provide detailed explanations. Frequent lyrics add to enjoyment for singing as well as to assist with rhythm.

~*~

SONGS

BANJO IN THE HOLLOW

TRADITIONAL

G tuning: gDGBD

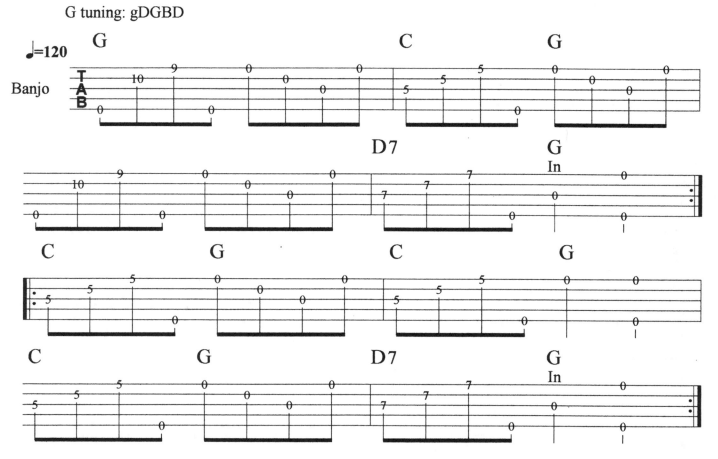

NOTES: (1) A series of forward/backward rolls make up this delightful
song, a favorite with students.

2) Don't let the high frets scare you. Think of the first roll as
a "10/9" chord. Try to have your fingers come down at the same
time rather than separately.

(3) The groups of 5s and 7s should be played as a 3-string barre
across the 1st, 2nd, and 3rd strings. You could barre all
strings but it takes more finger pressure.

(4) Both sections of the song are repeated.

(5) To avoid "double thumbing" use an index finger (marked
"In") for the single notes on the 3rd string before the pinch.

BILE 'EM CABBAGE DOWN

G tuning: gDGBD

TRADITIONAL

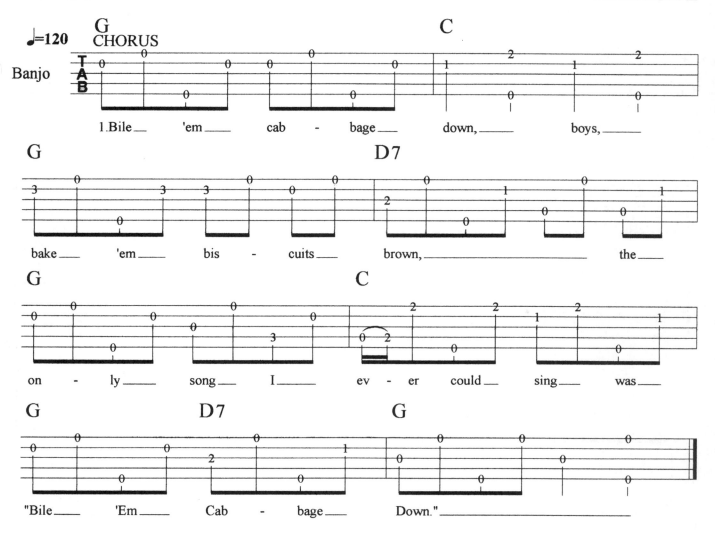

2. Once I had a muley cow,
   Her name was Bossy Brown,
   Ev'ry tooth in that cow's head was
   Forty inches 'round. CHORUS

3. Went up to the mountain top,
   Gave my horn a blow,
   Thought I heard my true love say,
   "Yonder comes my beau." CHORUS

4. Raccoon up a cinnamon tree,
   Possum on the ground,
   Possum says to the old raccoon,
   "Won't you throw some cinnamons down." CHORUS

COTTON-EYE JOE

G tuning: gDGBD

TRADITIONAL

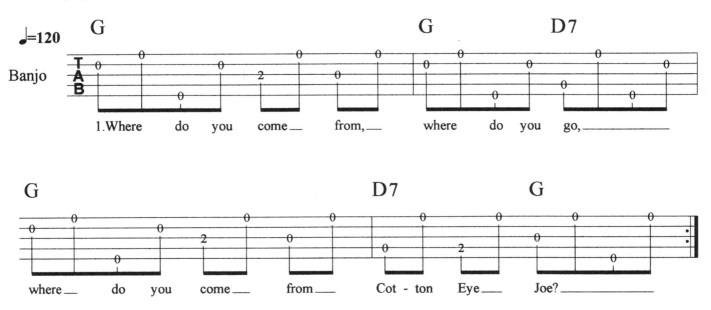

Verse 2: Come for to see you, come for to sing,
Come for to show you my diamond ring.

NOTES: (1) This song uses 4-note rolls and several lead/answers.
(2) The 4-note rolls have a heavy line at the bottom (called a beam) that connects the four notes.
(3) The lead/answers have just two notes and they are connected at the bottom with a heavy beam line.
(4) Accompaniment chord symbols are shown. Two of the measures are "split" and require two different chords.
(5) There's a repeat sign at the end of the song that directs you back to the beginning to play the song again.

CRIPPLE CREEK

G tuning: gDGBD

TRADITIONAL

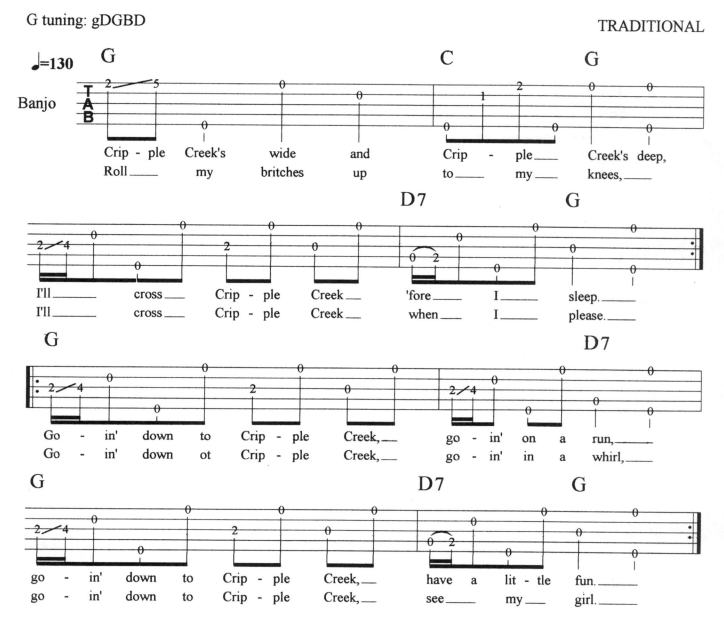

NOTES: (1) A diagonal line is used to indicate a slide from one note to another. The first slide marked with a single beam is slow. The other slides marked with a double bean are played faster.

(2) The arch over two notes is a hammer-on. The notes are joined with a double beam and are played fast.

(3) There are two sections of the song and each section is repeated.

(4) The song "Cotton-Eye Joe" can be substituted for the second section.

(5) Several measure are "split" with two different chords.

CUMBERLAND GAP

G tuning: gDGBD

TRADITIONAL

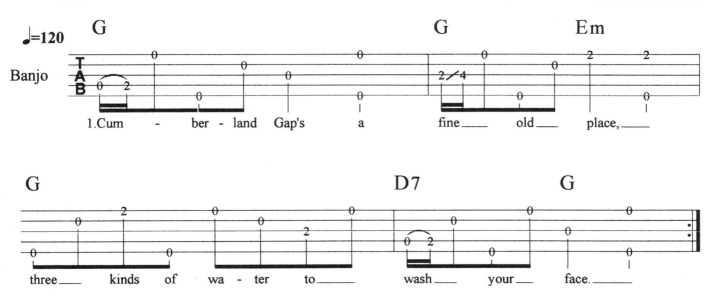

2nd Verse: Lay down, boys, take a little nap,
            Fourteen miles to Cumberland Gap.

3rd Verse: Me and my wife and my wife's pap,
            We all went down to Cumberland Gap

NOTES: This little song is loaded with techniques.

(1) The first measure starts with a hammer-on 4-note roll followed by a single note and a pinch.

(2) The second measures starts with a sliding 4-note roll followed by a single note and a pinch.

(3) The third measure combines a forward roll with a backward roll.

(4) The fourth measure is just like the first measure except that it changes the string order of the roll to L-2-5-1.

(5) The accompaniment chords are split in the second and last measures. The first split introduces the Em chord.

(6) A repeat sign at the end of the last measure directs you back to the beginning to play the song again.

GROUND HOG

G tuning: gDGBD

TRADITIONAL

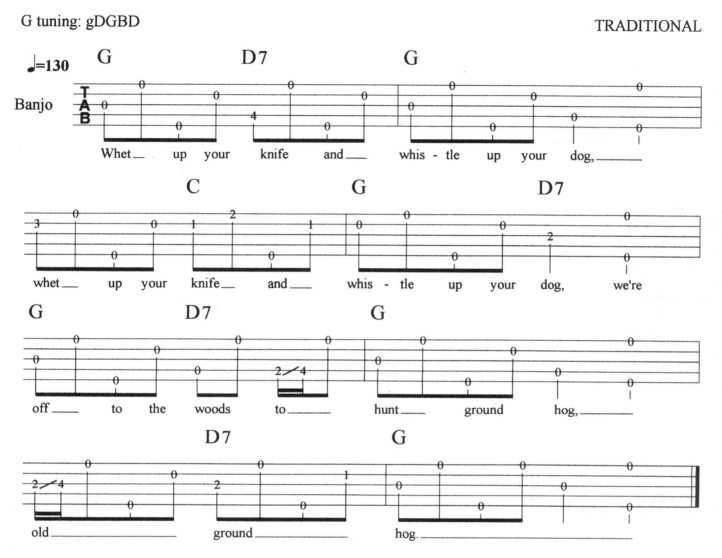

NOTES: (1) G tuning is indicated with the letters gDGBD. The small "g" refers to the high pitched "g" of the 5th string.

(2) Chord symbols are shown for accompaniment. There are several split measures where two chords are played in one measure.

(3) This song uses 4-note rolls (one with a sliding lead), several single notes and pinches, and a sliding lead/answer. Can you spot them all?

HANDSOME MOLLY

G tuning: gDGBD

TRADITIONAL

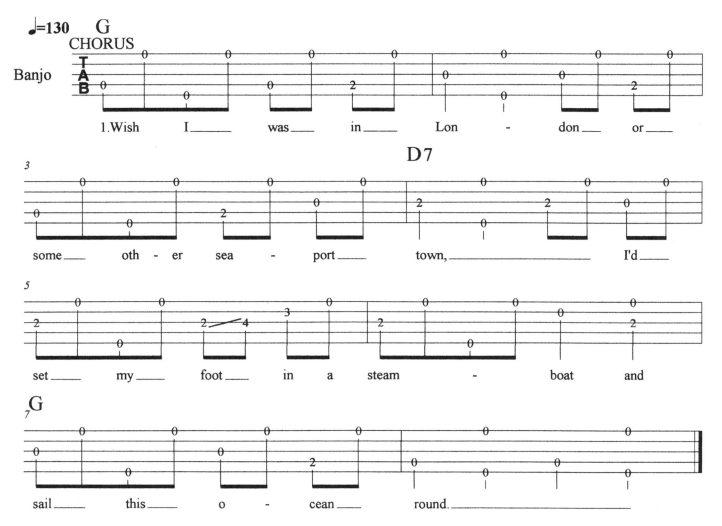

2. She rode to church on Sunday, she passed me on by,
   I could tell her mind was changing by the roving of her eye. CHORUS

3. Don't you remember, Molly, you gave me your right hand?
   Said if you'd ever marry that I would be your man. CHORUS

4. Now you've broke your promise, go home with whom you please,
   While my sad heart is aching you're lying at your ease. CHORUS

NOTES: (1) This song is in the 2-Finger banjo style. Only the thumb and index
       (or middle) fingers of the right hand are used.
       (2) Both verse and chorus have the same melody.
       (3) The slide in measure 5 is slow.
       (4) The pinch in measure 6 is played with the thumb and index fingers.

JOHNNY BOOKER

G tuning: gDGBD

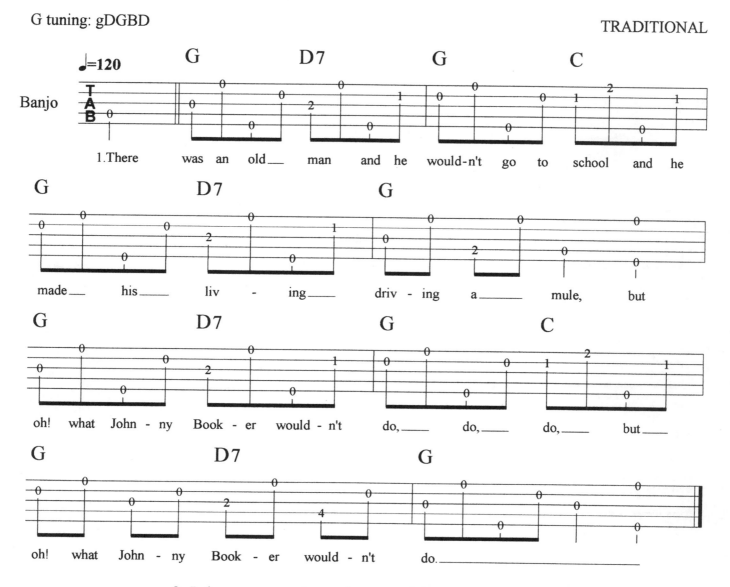

2. I drove my mule to the top of the hill,
   I hollered at him but the mule stood still,
   But oh! what Johnny Booker wouldn't do, do, do,
   But oh! what Johnny Booker wouldn't do.

NOTES: (1) All of the chords used in this song can be played with just
two fingers.
(2) Keep your fingers nimble and try making chord changes
quickly.
(3) The answering note of lead/answer is usually the 1st string
but other strings can be used as in the next to last measure.
(4) A double bar line is used to separate the pick-up note from
the main body of the song.

LITTLE BIRDIE

G tuning: gDGBD

TRADITIONAL

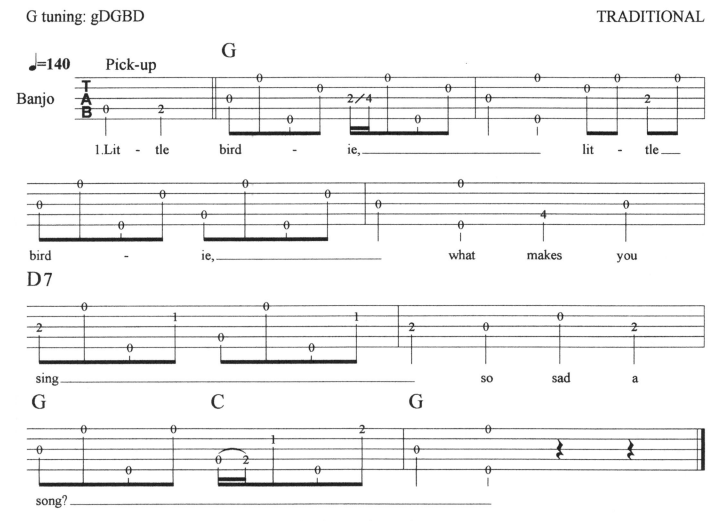

2. I've a short time
   For to be here
   And a long time
   To be gone.

NOTES: (1) The song starts with a pick-up of two notes. A pick-up is an incomplete measure that gives a running start to the song. In this song the pick-up is separated from the main body of the song by two vertical lines.
(2) In the final measure there are two 1-beat rests that look something like sea gulls. These rests would be filled in with the two pick-up notes if the song were to be sung again with the 2nd verse.
(3) If the song is not sung again substitute a single note and a pinch for the two rests.

SALT CREEK

TRADITIONAL

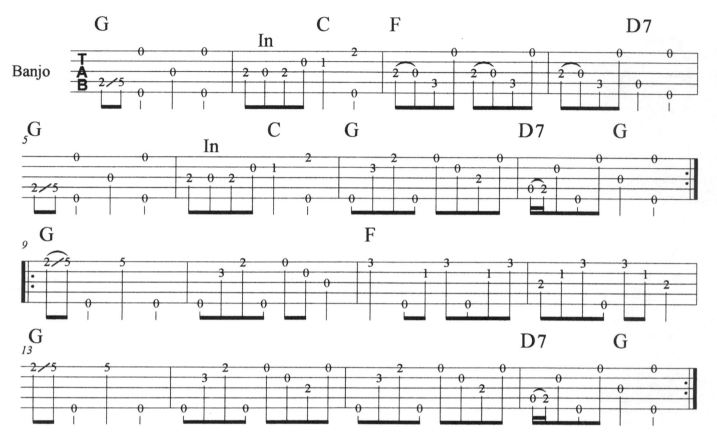

NOTES: (1) There are a number of slides in this song indicated by a slanted line between two notes.

(2) The last measure of each section has a 4-note roll with a string order of L-2-5-1 where the lead is a hammer-on.

(3) The use of an F chord in the key of G creates a "modal" sound often heard in Irish music. This lowering from G chord to an F chord can be called a "modal drop."

(4) Forward/backward rolls are found in measures 7, 14, and 15. The ones in measures 10 and 12 have an incomplete backward roll.

(5) In measures 2 and 6 the first open note is played with the index finger indicated with an "In".

(6) The pull-offs in measures 3 and 4 are played slowly.

SKIP TO MY LOU

G tuning: gDGBD

TRADITIONAL

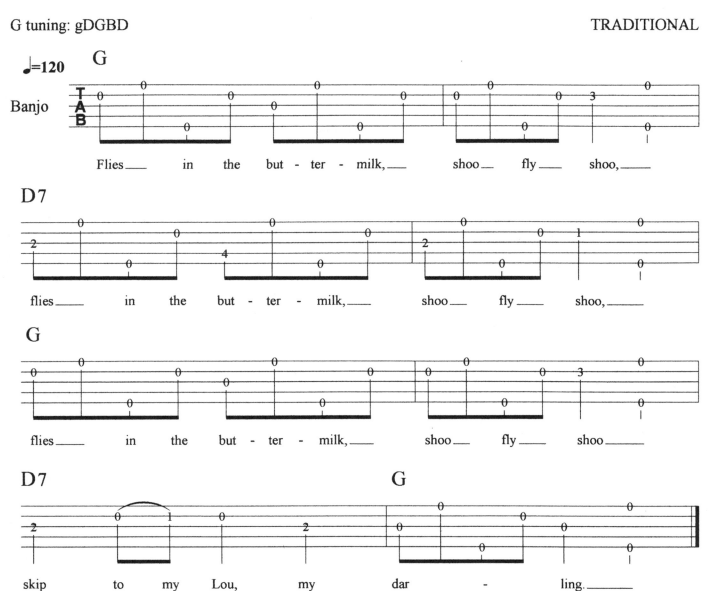

NOTES: (1) All of these 4-note rolls could be played with just the thumb
and middle (or index) index fingers in what's called a 2-finger
style.
(2) For a variation try changing the 4-note string order to L-1-5-1.
(3) The next to last measure has a slow hammer-on.

SOURWOOD MOUNTAIN

G tuning: gDGBD

TRADITIONAL

♩=120

Banjo

1. Chick-ens are a - crow - in' on Sour - wood Mount - ain,
So man - y pret - ty girls, I can't count em',

Hey, ho, did - dle um day.

2. My true love's a blue - eyed dai - sy,
I can't have her I'll go cra - zy,

Hey, ho, did - dle um day. (If)

3. My true love lives over the river,
Hey, ho, etc
A few more jumps and I'll be with her,
Hey, ho, etc.

4. Ducks in the pond and geese in the ocean,
Hey, ho, etc.
Devil's in a woman if they take a notion,
Hey, ho, etc.

SECTION TWO

All previous rolls and techniques are included in this section. Now the basic 8-note roll makes its first appearance. There's a well- known gospel hymn and an up-the-neck song that stretches to the limits of the high frets. You'll find another hymn modified and popularized by the Carter Family that has become something of a bluegrass anthem. For added interest and variety there's even a song with a built-in key change from G to C.

~*~

SONGS

Jim Mills

41

FIRE ON THE MOUNTAIN

G tuning: gDGBD

TRADITIONAL

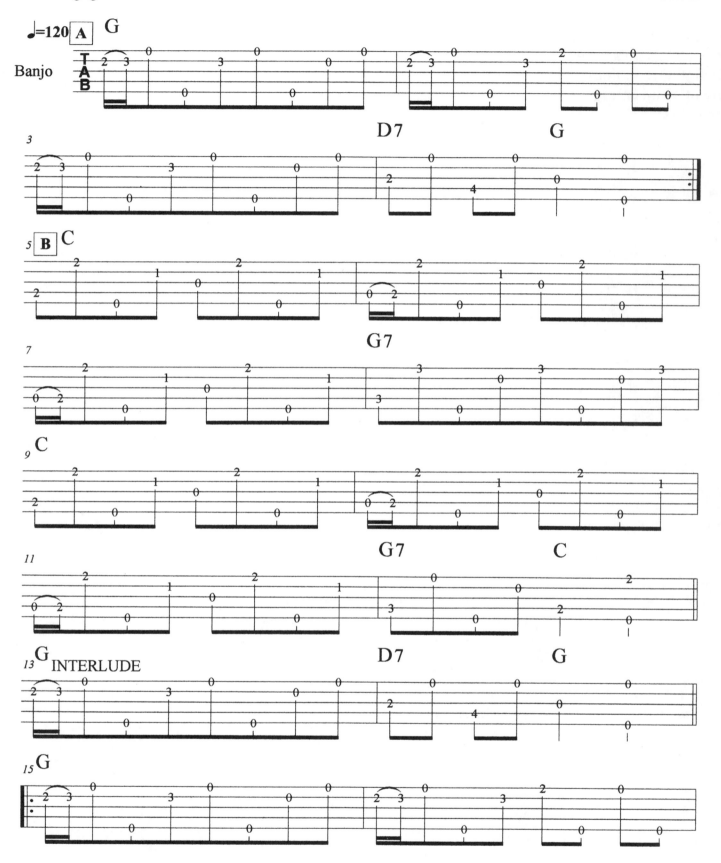

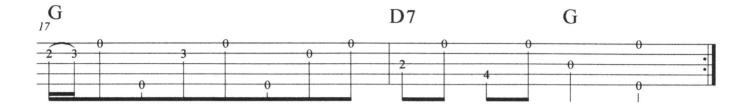

NOTES: (1) The A section is in the key of G. The B section is in the key of C.
(2) The "Interlude" acts as a transition from the B section back to the A section.
(3) The G7 chord can be formed by adding to the open G chord either the 3rd fret of the 4th string or the 3rd fret of the 1st string, or both.
(4) Notice in measures 1 and 3 that the 8-note roll lowers the next to last note from a 3rd fret to an open.
(5) The song sequence is: A 2 times, B 1 time, Interlude, A 2 times. Add a tag if you like.

John Hartford

IN THE SWEET BY AND BY

G tuning: gDGBD

SANFORD FILLMORE BENNETT

JOSEPH PHILBRICK WEBSTER

Gospel music, both vocal and instrumental, is a vital part of bluegrass.

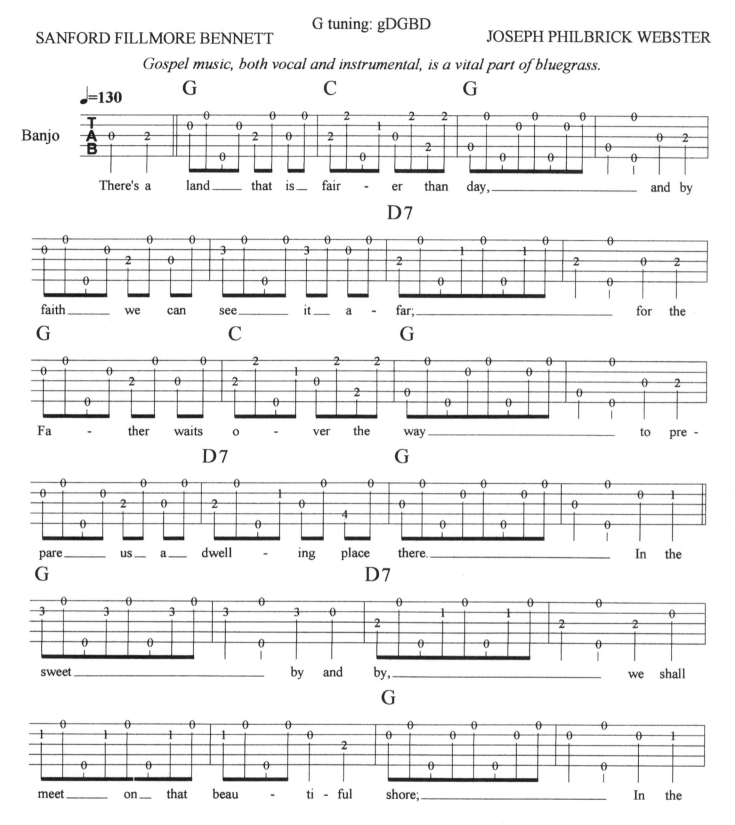

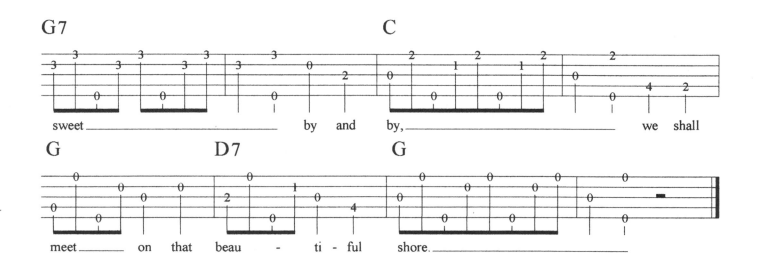

sweet _____ by and by, _____ we shall

meet _____ on that beau - ti - ful shore. _____

Derek Byrne

KEEP YOUR SKILLET GOOD AND GREASY

G tuning: gDGBD

TRADITIONAL

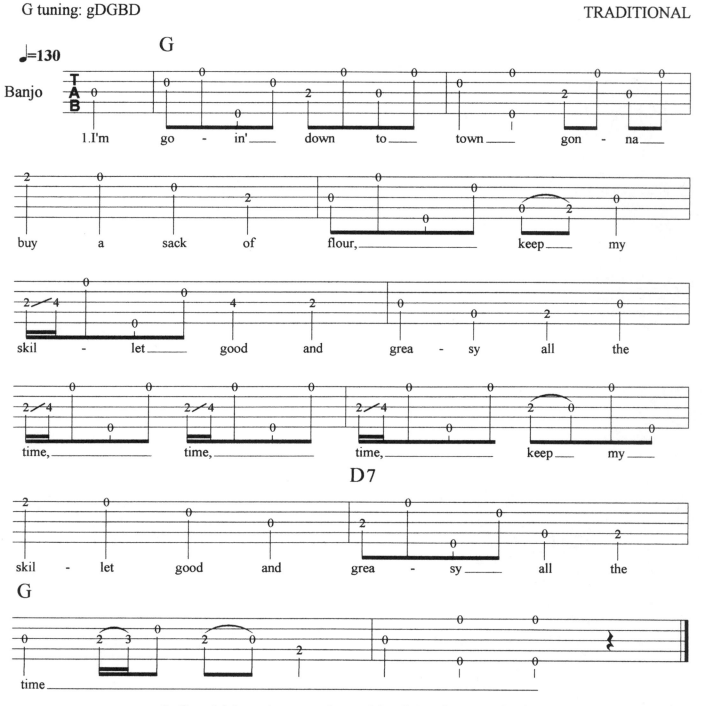

2. Got chickens in my sack, got bloodhounds on my back
   Gonna keep my skillet greasy all the time, time, time,
   Gonna keep my skillet greasy all the time.

3. I'm goin' down the street just to buy me a ham of meat,
   Gonna keep my skillet greasy ... Etc.

4. Oh, the times are very hard, gonna buy ten cents of lard,
   Gonna keep my skillet greasy ... Etc.

SALTY DOG

G tuning: gDGBD

TRADITIONAL

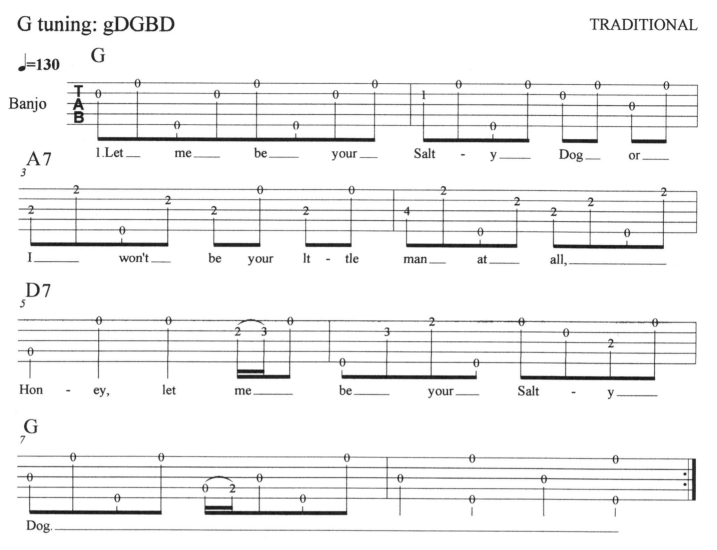

2. Standing on the corner with ther lowdown blues,
   Great big holes in the soles of my shoes,
   Honey, let me be your Salty Dog.

3. Pulled the trigger and the gun went go,
   Shot was heard down in Mexico,
   Honey, let me be your Salty Dog.

NOTES: (1) Starting with an 8-note roll, the song is loaded with lead/answers,
basic Scruggs rolls, a forward/backward roll, and two fast hammer-ons.
(2) Measures 3 and 4 are drawn from the A7 chord played by barring
the 2nd fret and overiding it with a 4th fret at the beginning of measure 4.
(3) The repeat sign at the end of measure 8 directs you back to the start
of the song. No forward repeat sign is necessary if the song goes
back to the beginning.

SUGAR HILL

G tuning: gDGBD

TRADITIONAL

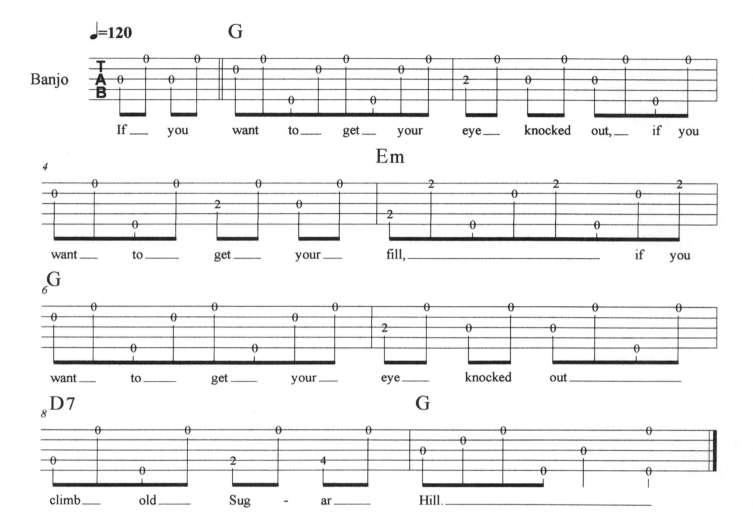

NOTES: (1) The double bar line ay the beginning separates the pick-up from the main body of the song.

(2) With the exception of the forward roll in the last measure, all the 4-note rolls and lead/answers are played 2-finger style with just the thumb and middle (or index) fingers.

(3) Eight-note rolls can be found in measures 2, 5, and 6.

(4) Bluegrass Rule: When playing fast don't use the same finger twice. In the final measure the forward roll ends with a thumb. Use an index finger for the single note instead of a thumb. This prevents "double thumbing."

(5) If notes are played slowly use of the same finger can be repeated. (See Breaks 3 and 5 in the *Intro, Breaks, Fills and Tags* section and *Banks Of The O-Hi-O* in Section Three.)

WEST LAKE BREAKDOWN

G tuning: gDGBD

DICK SHERIDAN

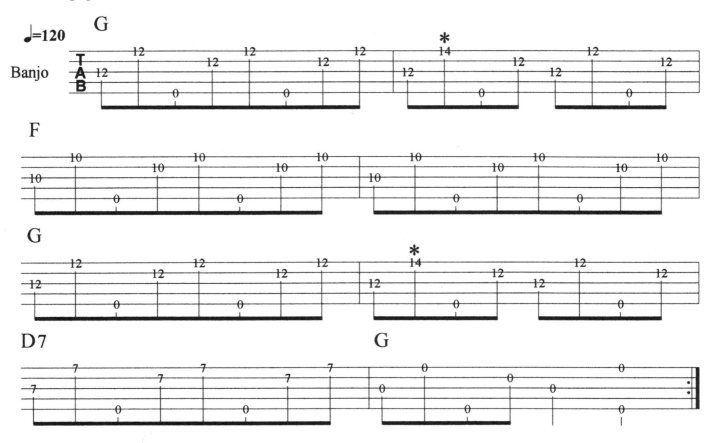

NOTES: (1) Upper frets can be daunting but don't let this up-the-neck song throw you. They're all 3-string barres played on the 12 fret, 10th fret, and 5th fret.
(2) There's an "override" of the 12th fret barre marked with an asterisk. Continue to hold the barre with the 1st finger, then with the ring finger add and release the override note on the 14th fret.
(3) Dropping from the G chord (12th fret) to the F chord (10th fret) creates a distinct modal sound.

WILL THE CIRCLE BE UNBROKEN

G tuning: gDGBD

TRADITIONAL

The Carter Family recorded this song in 1935 with lyrics reworked from the original hymn as a gloomy funeral song. This upbeat chorus, however, has become a blue-grass anthem and is frequently played at festivals and musical gatherings.

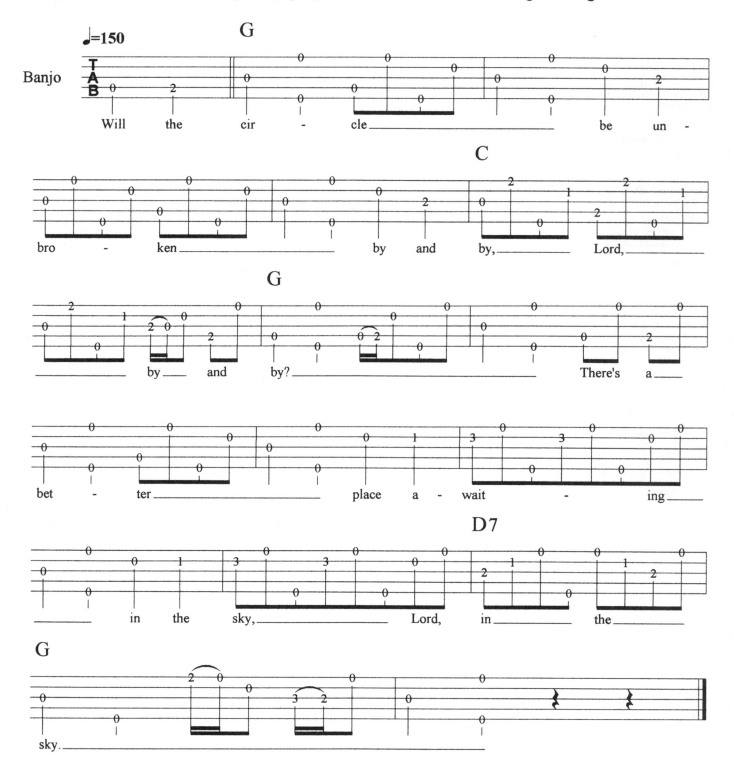

SECTION THREE

This section includes all previous material. In addition there are modal sounding songs, an introduction to 3/4 time, and several variations of 8-note rolls called spread, interrupted and cascading. Three new tunings are also introduced:

D tuning

C tuning

Modal tuning

~*~

SONGS

ALL THE GOOD TIMES ARE PAST AND GONE

G tuning: gDGBD

TRADITIONAL

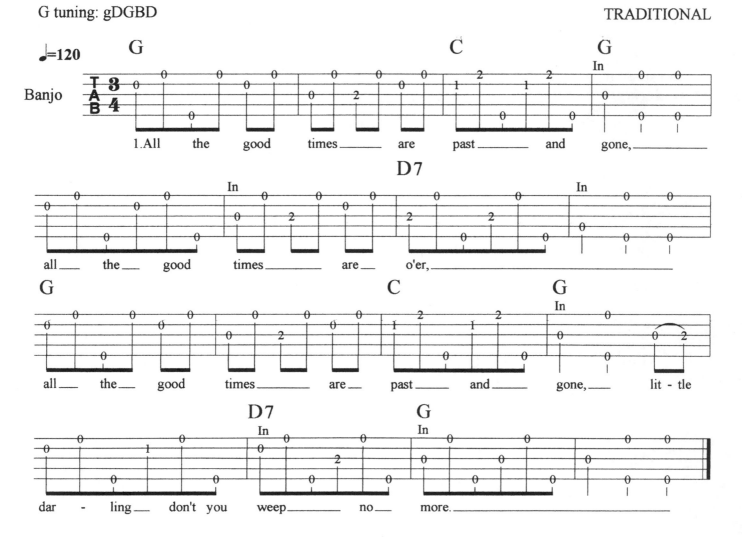

2. Come back, come back, my own true love
   And stay a while with me,
   If ever I've had a friend in the world,
   You've been a friend to me.

NOTES: There's a rule in bluegrass that the same right hand finger cannot
   be used twice when playing fast.   Since several of these fast
   6-note rolls end with the thumb, the thumb cannot be used again.
   An index finger indicated with an "In" must be substituted. This
   also requires the index finger to play strings lower than its usual
   2nd string.
   This song is in 3/4 time meaning 3 beats to the measure.

BANKS OF THE O-HI-O

C tuning: gCGBD

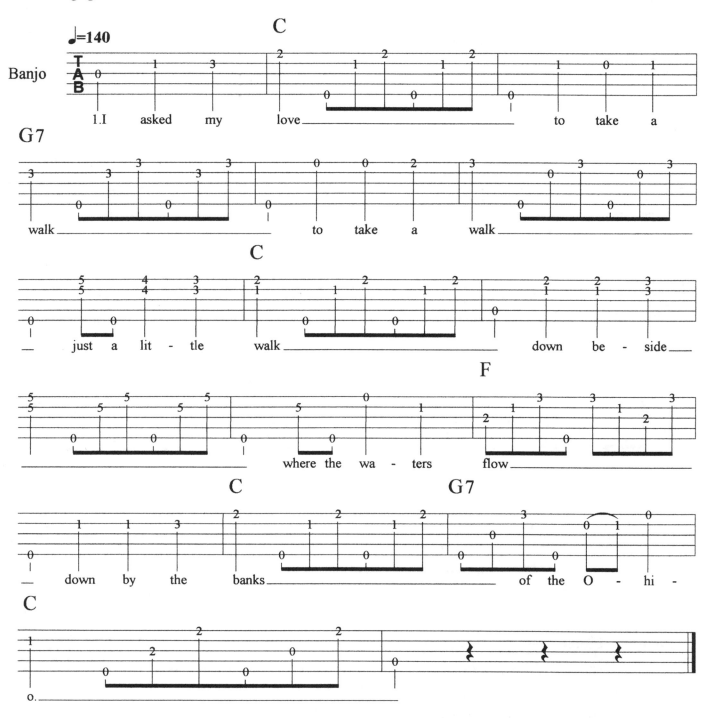

2. Then only say that you'll be mine
And in no other arms entwine,
Down by the banks where the waters flow,
Down by the banks of the O-hi-o.

BLACK MOUNTAIN RAG

G tuning: gDGBD

TRADITIONAL

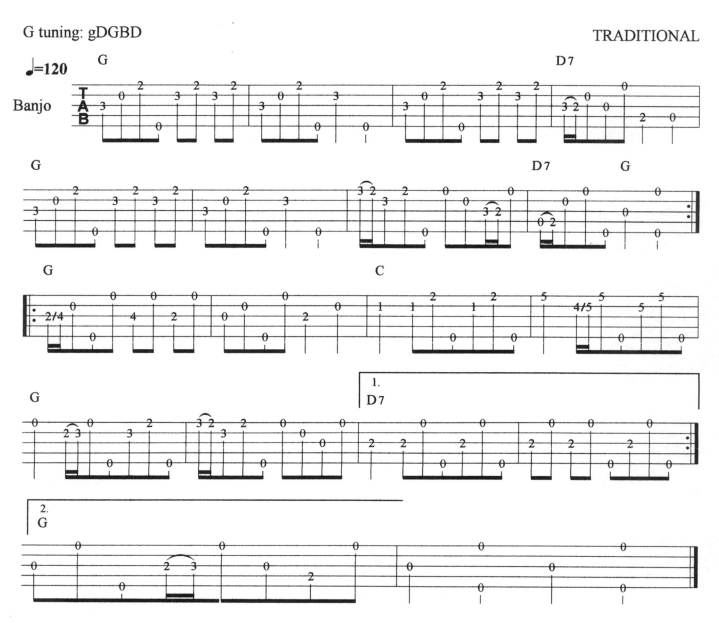

Notes: There two sections to this song and each section is repeated. The
frst repeat sign is called a "backward" repeat sign and directs you
backward to the beginning of song.

The next repeat sign is a "forward" repeat. It responds to the second
backward repeat sign and propels the song forward one more time.
The second section has a 1st and 2nd ending. Play the 1st ending
up to the repeat sign. When the song repeats skip the 1st ending
and play the 2nd endng instead.

DISTANT THUNDER

G tuning: gDGBD

DICK SHERIDAN

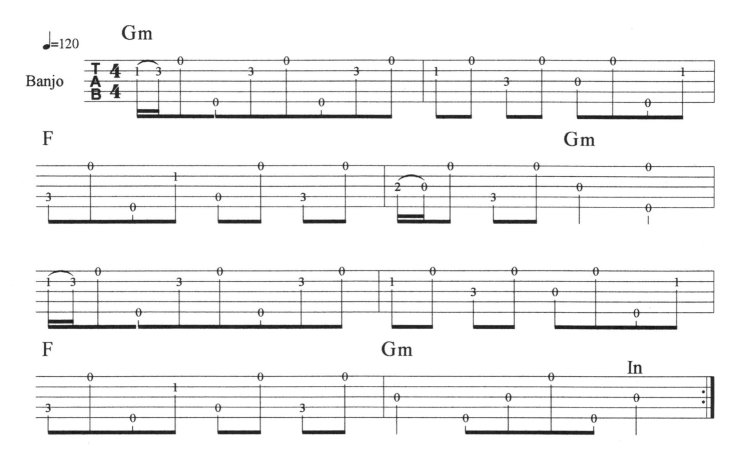

NOTE: (1) The sound of this song is modal, but instead of going to a modal tuning (gDGCD), hold down the 1st fret of the 2nd string which produces the C note of modal tuning. For a more "lonesome" sound, try substituting a G major chord for the G minor.

(2) In the last measure the forward roll ends with a thumb. To avoid fast "double thumbing" use and index finger (marked "In") for the final single note. Using two thumbs at the beginning of the last measure is okay since the single note is slow allowing ample time for the thumb to advance to the forward roll.

OLD JOE CLARK

G tuning: gDGBD

TRADITIONAL

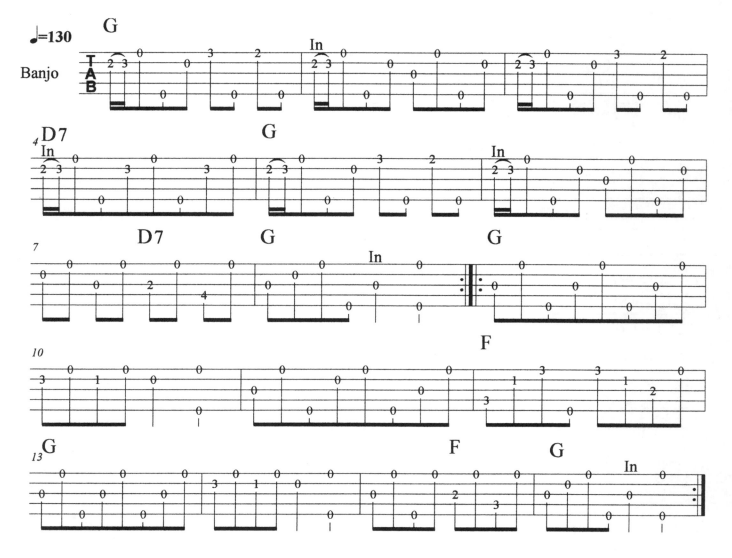

NOTES: (1) The lead/answers in measures 1, 3, and 5 are reversed with the lead on the 1st string and the answer on the 5th.

(2) There are a number of places where the index finger should follow the thumb to avoid "double thumbing." These are marked with an "In".

(3) There are "spread" 8-note rolls in measures 9, 11, and 13 where the index finger leaves the 2nd string and plays the 3rd.

LITTLE MAGGIE

G tuning: gDGBD

TRADITIONAL

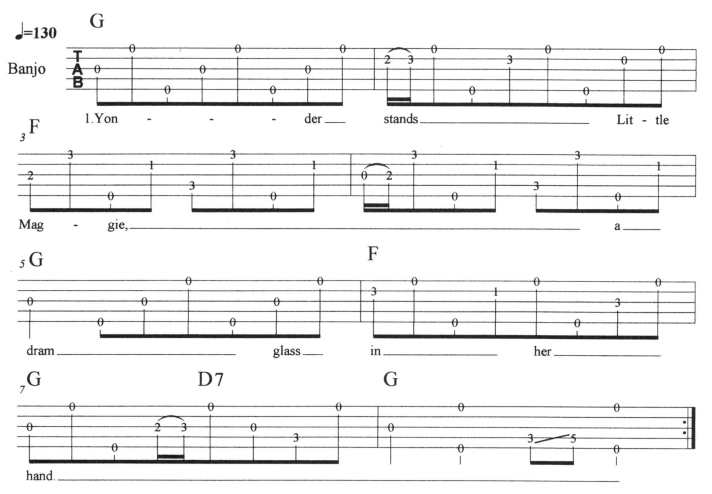

2. She's drinking away all her troubles,
   Hanging 'round with some other man.

3. Last time I seen Little Maggie,
   She was sitting on the banks by the sea.

4. Had a pistol tied to her body,
   And a banjo on her knee.

NOTES: (1) Although not precisely modal, *Little Maggie* certainly has
a modal sound with the "drop-modal" F chord.
(2) Measure 5 has an interrupted roll pattern, while Measure 6
could be called a "cascading" 8-note roll because of the descending tumble of notes.
(3) Measure 7 is often used as a break and is a classic fill.
(4) A backward repeat sign brings you back to the beginning.

RAILROAD BILL

G tuning: gDGBD

TRADITIONAL

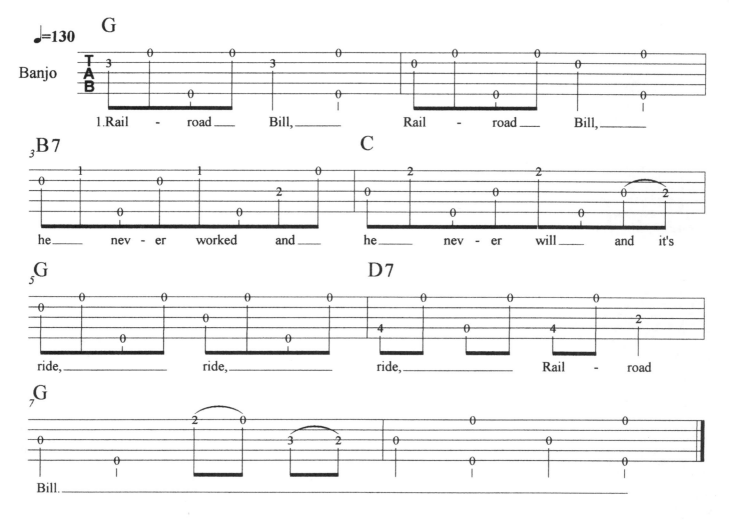

2. Railroad Bill's a mighty mean man,
   Shot the lantern from the brakeman's hand,
   And it's ride, ride, ride, Railroad Bill.

3. Got me a pistol long as my arm,
   Shoot anybody ever done me harm,
   And it's ride, ride, ride Railroad Bill.

NOTES: (1) The hammer-on in measure 4 and the pull-offs in measure 7 are played slow.

(2) Measure 3 has a "cascading" 8-note roll where the melody drops down within the roll.

(3) Measure 4 has a "spread" 8-note roll where the index finger plays the 3rd string instead of usually playing the 2nd.

(4) The slow pull-offs in measure 7 are "fills" and not part of the melody.

REUBEN
(Reuben's Train)

D tuning: f#DF#AD

TRADITIONAL

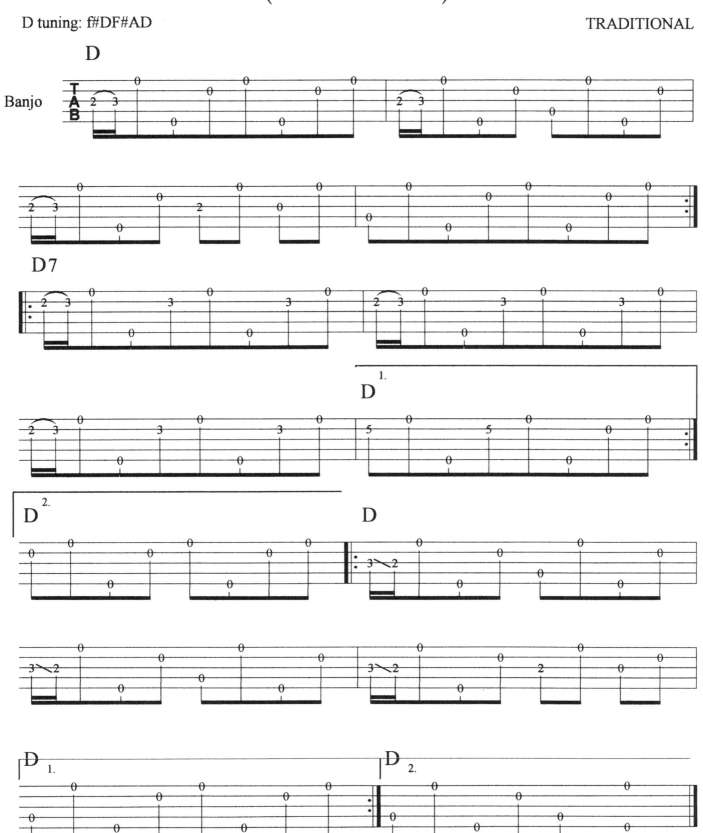

SHADY GROVE

G modal tuning: gDGCD

TRADITIONAL

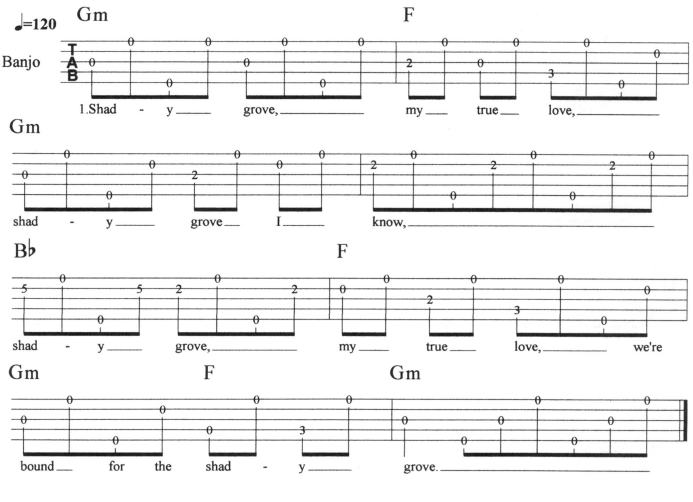

2. Peaches in the summertime,
   Apples in the fall,
   If I can't have the one I love
   I won't have none at all.

NOTES: G modal tuning is known by several other names such as
Sawmill tuning and Mountain Minor tuning. It raises the
2nd string from a B to a C. Songs in modal tuning can be
somewhat unsettling -- they're not quite major and they're
not quite minor. Another modal song, *Little Maggie,*
is included in this section. Other modal songs you might
like to check out online are *Frosty Morning, Pretty Polly,*
and *The Cuckoo.*

TOM DOOLEY

G tuning: gDGBD

2. Met her on the moutain,
There I took her life,
Met her on the mountain,
Stabbed her with my knife.

3. This time tomorrow,
Reckon where I'd be,
If it hadn't been for Grayson
I'd-a been in Tennessee.

NOTES: (1) The second measure is an 8-note roll that starts off with a sliding lead.

(2) Measure 7 has a pull-off lead/answer.

WILDWOOD FLOWER

G tuning: gDGBD

TRADITIONAL

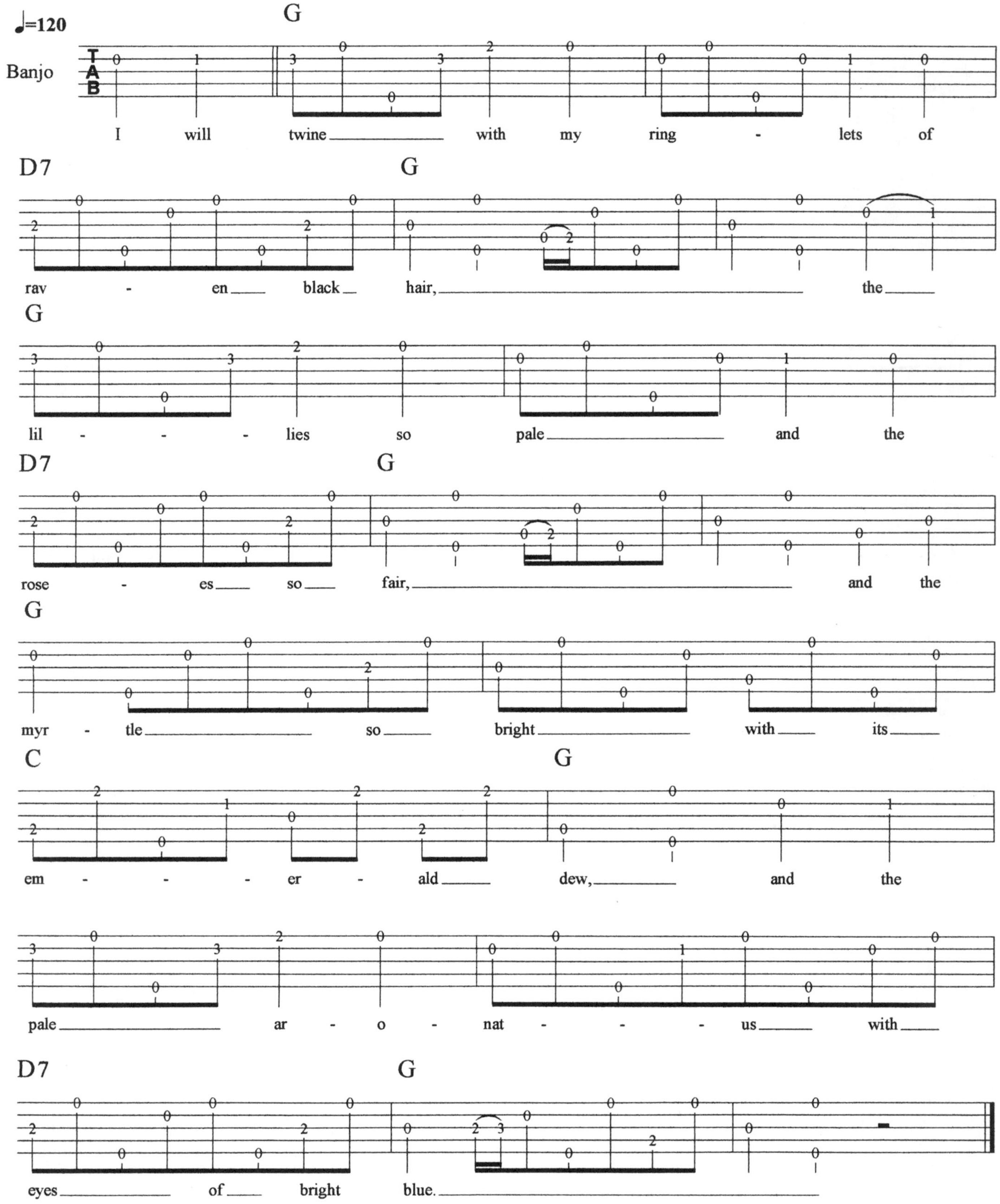

More Great Banjo Books from Centerstream...

BEGINNING CLAWHAMMER BANJO
 DVD

by Ken Perlman

Ken Perlman is one of the most celebrated clawhammer banjo stylists performing today. In this new DVD, he teaches how to play this exciting style, with ample close-ups and clear explanations of techniques such as: hand positions, chords, tunings, brush-thumb, single-string strokes, hammer-ons, pull-offs and slides. Songs include: Boatsman • Cripple Creek • Pretty Polly. Includes a transcription booklet. 60 minutes.

00000330 DVD $19.95

INTERMEDIATE CLAWHAMMER BANJO
DVD

by Ken Perlman

Picking up where *Beginning Clawhammer Banjo* leaves off, this DVD begins with a review of brush thumbing and the single-string stroke, then moves into specialized techniques such as: drop- and double-thumbing, single-string brush thumb, chords in double "C" tuning, and more. · Tunes include: Country Waltz • Green Willis • Little Billie Wilson • Magpie • The Meeting of the Waters • Old Joe Clark • and more! Includes a transcription booklet. 60 minutes.

00000331 DVD $19.95

CLAWHAMMER STYLE BANJO
INCLUDES TAB DVD

A Complete Guide for Beginning and Advanced Banjo Players

by Ken Perlman

This handbook covers basic right & left-hand positions, simple chords, and fundamental clawhammer techniques: the brush, the "bumm-titty" strum, pull-offs, and slides. There is also instruction on more complicated picking, double thumbing, quick slides, fretted pull-offs, harmonics, improvisation, and more. Includes over 40 fun-to-play banjo tunes.

00000118 Book Only $19.95
00000334 DVD $39.95

THE EARLY MINSTREL BANJO
INCLUDES TAB

by Joe Weidlich

Featuring more than 65 classic songs, this interesting book teaches how to play the minstrel banjo like players who were part of various popular troupes in 1865. The book includes: a short history of the banjo, including the origins of the minstrel show; info on the construction of minstrel banjos; chapters on each of the seven major banjo methods published through the end of the Civil War; songs from each method in banjo tablature, many available for the first time; info on how to arrange songs for the minstrel banjo; a reference list of contemporary gut and nylon string gauges approximating historical banjo string tensions in common usage during the antebellum period (for those Civil War re-enactors who wish to achieve that old-time "minstrel banjo" sound); an extensive cross-reference list of minstrel banjo song titles found in the major antebellum banjo methods; and more. (266 pages)

00000325 .... $29.95

MELODIC CLAWHAMMER BANJO

A Comprehensive Guide to Modern Clawhammer Banjo

by Ken Perlman

Ken Perlman, today's foremost player of the style, brings you this comprehensive guide to the melodic clawhammer. Over 50 tunes in clear tablature. Learn to play authentic versions of Appalachian fiddle tunes, string band tunes, New England hornpipes, Irish jigs, Scottish reels, and more. Includes arrangements by many important contemporary players, and chapters on basic and advanced techniques. Also features over 70 musical illustrations, plus historical notes, and period photos.

00000412 Book/CD Pack $19.95

MINSTREL BANJO – BRIGGS' BANJO INSTRUCTOR
INCLUDES TAB

by Joseph Weidlich

The Banjo Instructor by Tom Briggs, published in 1855, was the first complete method for banjo. It contained "many choice plantation melodies," "a rare collection of quaint old dances," and the "elementary principles of music." This edition is a reprinting of the original Briggs' *Banjo Instructor*, made up-to-date with modern explanations, tablature, and performance notes. It teaches how to hold the banjo, movements, chords, slurs and more, and includes 68 banjo solo songs that Briggs presumably learned directly from slaves.

00000221 .... $12.95

MORE MINSTREL BANJO
INCLUDES TAB

by Joseph Weidlich

This is the second book in a 3-part series of intabulations of music for the minstrel (Civil War-era) banjo. Adapted from Frank Converse's *Banjo Instructor, Without a Master* (published in New York in 1865), this book contains a choice collection of banjo solos, jigs, songs, reels, walk arounds, and more, progressively arranged and plainly explained, enabling players to become proficient banjoists. Thorough measure-by-measure explanations are provided for each of the songs, all of which are part of the traditional minstrel repertoire.

00000258 .... $12.95

WITH MY BANJO ON MY KNEE

The Minstrel Songs of Stephen Foster
arr. for banjo by Daniel Partner
Historical notes by Edwin J. Sims

Here are some of the first and most popular songs ever written for banjo. Fascinating historical notes accompany this collection, describing the meaning of the songs, their place in history, the significance of the musicians who first performed them, and Foster himself, America's first professional songwriter. The complete original lyrics of each song and an extensive bibliography are included. The CD contains recordings of each arrangement performed on solo minstrel banjo.

00001179 Book/CD Pack $19.95

P.O. Box 17878 - Anaheim Hills, CA 92817
(714) 779-9390   www.centerstream-usa.com